Airbnb Secrets Super-Host

Beginners Guide

By: Julie Landin

CLADD
PUBLISHING

Cladd Publishing Inc.
USA

This publication is designed to provide accurate information regarding the subject matter covered. It is sold with the understanding that neither the author nor the publisher is providing medical, legal or other professional advice or services. Always seek advice from a competent professional before using any of the information in this book. The author and the publisher specifically disclaim any liability that is incurred from the use or application of the contents of this book.

Airbnb Secrets Super-Host: Beginners Guide

ISBN 978-1-946881-37-3 (e-book)
ISBN 978-1-946881-38-0 (paperback)

Contents

Why Host on Airbnb

Anyone who has stayed at a hotel in the past decade knows it's not cheap. In fact, even basic hotel rooms will cost you around $100 a night. For a room with a nicer mattress in a better location, you could easily spend $200 or more.

There is a lot of money to be made in the lodging industry. And because of Airbnb, it's has become easier for the average person to get a slice of the pie.

Airbnb is a quality lodging option for travelers and a new way to make extra money for those who have space they can rent out.

Making Money Is Easy

If you have an empty house, apartment, tent, yard, treehouse or anything else someone can sleep in, then you are a shoe in. Airbnb handles all the money and takes a small cut of the transaction. This small-cut is well worth the burden it takes off its members backs.

How It Works

Airbnb involves sharing a personal property with travellers. This concept is based on the idea that part of the magic of traveling comes from feeling like you belong. By offering tourists a more immersive way to experience a destination, the founders of Airbnb have created a business that it's worth $30 billion and growing.

Airbnb is the most significant player in this niche market. It's active in over 190 countries and has over 60 million tourists as customers.

The original motivation was to supply a way for people with spare-room, to make a use of their empty places in times when the accommodation in the city was insufficient for the number of travellers. This was usually during festivals, concerts, conventions, holidays, or when hotels were offering overpriced services. However, Airbnb has become a top choice for all types of travellers, from short breaks tourists and backpackers to business people that are looking for an authentic experience.

If you're thinking of trying Airbnb, this comprehensive guide to insider's secrets, will give you everything you need to know about how to make top dollar, becoming a super host, and landing 5-star reviews from all of your guest.

Who Host on Airbnb?

Two types of people that host on Airbnb

1. Those who would like to earn extra income, in addition to their current career.
2. And those who would like to make hosting a full-time career.

Making your property, room, backyard, tent, hammock or couch available on Airbnb, could make you that income you have been wishing for.

However, while you may not be thinking of renting your home on a short-term basis as a business, it is. Whether you are listing your property just for extra income or working towards making it your primary source of income, you must treat it like a business if you want to succeed.

New Economy Trend

This fast-growing sharing-economy offers a way to make extra income that was not available before.

However, these opportunities require you to be comfortable navigating local laws, sharing your most valuable possessions with strangers, and taking on additional legal liability.

Unusual Ways to Make Money

Rent Out Anything

Airbnb is one of the only places you can rent temporary accommodations to travellers from all over the world. Accommodations don't necessarily mean just an entire home, or room. It could be your backyard or even a couch; the limits are endless.

Turning Spaces into Places

Many people are choosing to build out their garages into living spaces. This is also true with tree houses, and storage sheds. By turning the unused structures into liveable units, you can reap rental income for years to come.

RV, Trailers, and Tents

This type of rental works well in high demand places, where other accommodations are expensive. Set these units up with a grill, outdoor fire pit, restroom options (or an out-house), fishing poles, canoes, etc.

Be sure to park it in a location on your property that would provide privacy. You could even park it at a camp ground close by and let them stay there. The sky is the limit.

No Spare Room - No Worries

TEAM UP WITH A FRIEND

List one of your property on Airbnb. When you get a booking, stay with the other person and split the profits. Or list both properties and stay in the property that failed to rent. If both rent, stay with family/friend, hotel, sleep at your office, in your car, or at a campground.

PROFIT ON YOUR YARD

Do you have a beautiful yard? Then you could have a very profitable Airbnb listing.

Set up a nice tent, grill, outdoor lounging and tables, big screen tv, candles, and lights.

If you are lucky enough and have a pool, an outdoor fireplace or fire pit to roast marshmallows and hotdogs you could easily be booked all summer long. You can even offer wedding space or a stay in your tree house. **The ideas and potential income are endless.**

USE YOUR COUCH

You may not have an extra room, a spacious backyard, or a treehouse, but you likely have a couch. The CEO of Airbnb used to list his sofa sleeper for $50 per night.

This strategy works best in big cities or tourist destinations where accommodations are expensive, but it's an option anyone can try anywhere.

Short-term Rental Restrictions

City Rules

First, you should get informed about the legal context of house-sharing in your state and your city. Some cities have restrictions regarding the number of days and guests. While a few cities dictate the number of rooms, you can provide for tourists.

Get Permission

Before listing any part of your property, you may need to get permission. If an HOA or co-op control your property, check its rules to make sure you're allowed to rent on a short-term basis.

Get It in Writing

If you rent, you'll want to get your landlord's permission in writing. If you are looking for a property to rent for the specific purpose of hosting it on Airbnb, add a clause in your contract that allows you to do so.

Business License & Taxes

After you have verified that you are in good standing to rent your property, you must now understand the taxes you will be required to pay.

Hotel Tax

You most likely will have to pay a **transient occupancy tax**, the same tax that applies to hotels. Hotels commonly pass this fee onto their guests.

Before you do that same thing, check with the other Airbnb listings in your area, and try to follow their method of taxation. You do not want potential guest going someone else because you have a massive tax that will be applied on top of the listing price. You may want to include this tax in the listing price, so it is not seen.

Personal Income

You'll also owe federal taxes on Airbnb income, which will be reported to you and the IRS on a form called 1099. This revenue has not had taxes taken out prior to, so you will likely owe something.

However, you may be able to reduce your taxable Airbnb income by deducting expenses, such as cleaning fees, items purchased and insurance. Always seek tax advice from a tax professional.

Filing as a Business Entity

Filing your generated sales under a business entity such as an LLC (limited liability) will allow you a certain level of protection and deductions that are not otherwise possible. Speak to your local accountant or attorney for options that meet your individual needs.

Insurance Coverage and Claims

Most Airbnb guests are wonderful, but on a rare occasion, you could get a guest who is not so great. Thus, Airbnb has insurance coverage you can access, but you should carefully review what it covers.

Airbnb offers liability only insurance for U.S. hosts. Members could receive up to $1 million per occurrence. However, this is secondary to any other insurance you may already carry, such as your homeowner's, renter's or landlord's insurance coverage. Airbnb's liability insurance has conditions and limitations, so read the fine print thoroughly.

Airbnb's Guarantee

Airbnb's host guarantee doesn't protect against general wear and tear to your property or possessions, but you can charge a security deposit to cover those damages. You'll want to document any damage with photos and substantiate the "before" value of any damaged property.

How to File a Claim

Airbnb requires that hosts try to resolve any problems with guests directly before filing a claim. To file a claim with Airbnb for more than $300, you must first submit a police report within 14 days of the incident.

Talk to your homeowner's or renter's insurance company to make sure your policy will cover your property, your possessions, and your liability while renting out your place through Airbnb. If you need extra coverage, an umbrella policy might be the ticket. See Homeowner's Insurance Guide.

Keeping A Security Deposit

Airbnb provides an option to procure a refundable security deposit, which is very important for deterring unwanted behavior in the guest. If damage does occur outside of regular wear and tear, you can choose to file a reasonable claim against their security deposit.

Airbnb Host Requirements

To become a host, you first need to set up an account. Getting on Airbnb is free for both the hosts and the guests, and it can be quickly done using only your email address or your Facebook or Google+ account. Once you're all set up, the fun begins.

"Hospitality is the secret to success," is one of Airbnb's mottos. Therefore, to ensure that every experience is as best as it can be, there are several hosting standards that the company imposes on both hosts and guests. Once you have become a member, you must be ready to work hard to ensure that your hospitality gets highly rated reviews.

The Math Is Simple

Good reviews, means more guests; and more guests mean more money on Airbnb.

Theft

Is it safe to rent out your home to a stranger? If you are renting out your entire home, and you won't be there, you are usually not at risk of physical violence. However, you'll want to find a safe place to store anything sentimental or of financial value. Don't give guests the opportunity to steal your possessions or your identity.

If you have a garage that can be locked and secured, that is probably your best bet. Otherwise, renting a small storage unit or brining important items to a friend or family members home would be other options to consider. The worst-case scenario would be to store your belongings in a locked closet inside the home. But if this is all you have, its better then leaving items where guest can gain access.

Is Hosting on Airbnb Safe?

One question that everybody has regarding Airbnb is safety. Obviously, there is the risk that you may come across people who are neither kind nor respectful. There have been cases when Airbnb hosts faced extraordinary things: a house destroyed after a party, tourists who changed the locks and did not want to leave, etc.

Airbnb faced a PR crisis in 2011 regarding this issue when a renter's home was vandalized and robbed. The story reached all media outlets and became a disaster for membership. Since then, Airbnb has implemented a complex system that has become the standard in the house-sharing industry.

Fixing the Problem

To counteract the problem Airbnb's platform does not accept anonymity. Also, the review system now works both ways, allowing hosts to rate a guest. If renters or hosts get too many low remarks, they are suspended or given penalties. Reviews represent the most legitimate feedback about the host or the guest, and it motivates people to be respectful and to fulfil their responsibilities and obligations.

Taking Control

In addition, you can always decline a reservation or even cancel a booking, though in some cases Airbnb will impose penalties. A host has no obligation to accept a reservation request if they do not feel comfortable. If you need more information about a prospective guest, the platform has a Facebook Connect tool that allows hosts to request recommendations from friends.

You can also limit the reservations you accept to guests who have completed Airbnb's Verified ID process. Both hosts and guests can have Airbnb verify their identity by uploading a valid government-issued ID and connecting a Facebook, Google+ or LinkedIn account to an Airbnb account.

Before a reservation is booked, parties can communicate only through the Airbnb platform. By doing so, Airbnb can keep an eye on the closed communication between hosts and guests and ensure that everything remains safe and secure. Also, both the renter and guest are screened through authorized and verified credit card information.

After the reservation is booked, parties are given contact information so that they can communicate with ease.

Secure Payments

Payments are secured through online banking methods. When a guest books a reservation, they must provide their credit card information to ensure that the host will get paid.

Other Payment Methods

Airbnb offers international banking transfer through a PayPal account, or money transfer services. The payment is made a day after the guest has arrived at your property.

How to Be a Top-Rated Host

To be considered a top-rated host on Airbnb is not as difficult as you may think. Take some time to get in the minds of a guest, and even pretend to look for a place to stay. This exercise will open your eyes to the things you may be doing wrong, innovative ways to attract a guest and much more.

Increase Your Ratings

Below is a list of ways that top-rated hosts earn their stars.

- Innovative descriptions and pictures.

- Quick response times.

- Super cleanliness.

- Providing your guests with local information.

- Directions from the airport, or picking them up.

- Handling key exchanges promptly.

- Providing at least one happy surprise.

- Offer superior customer service.

- Make their stay comfortable and relaxing.

Check Your Account

The best hosts will check their account hourly. While less successful hosts take days to respond, and rarely update their calendar. There is a vast difference in customer service from the guest's perspective. The faster your response time, the happier the guest will be with their initial experience. This automatically sets the stage for a better relationship and ultimately a higher rating.

Cleaning

Find a cleaning service that has good availability and that you can schedule via text message or email. Try to find a service that can bring their own cleaning supplies and a team of cleaners for a faster turn-around time. Its not ideal to hire one person that will need an entire day to clean, and may not be available right away.

Key Exchange

Consider installing a smart lock or a lockbox. This small tip alone will save you a lot of time waiting for your guests.

Due to the nature of traveling, your guest can often be late. If you're not comfortable with that, consider paying a neighbour to handle keys for you.

Welcome Package

Make a welcome package for your guest, with details and operating instructions of your property. Don't forget to include your internet password, along with how to turn on appliances like the A/C or heater.

Include all the dates for conferences, shows, outdoor adventures and big events in your city.

Complete Profile 100%

Complete all verifications and fields in your profile, so Airbnb rewards you with a better place in their search results.

Update your listing regularly

Airbnb is not like Craigslist; it is not an electric bulletin board. It's more like an active/live matchmaker. They try to help users quickly find a hotel alternative that suits them best in real time. Airbnb is always adding categories to describe amenities and neighborhoods better. You must routinely update your listing's description, or be at risk of getting pushed behind hosts that do.

Invest in a calendar book

A good calender book is probably one of the most overlooked parts of running a successful hosting business. You must be documenting all bookings, in-out times, key arrangements, scheduled cleanings, maintenance, call backs, and emails in one single place. Having your calendar allows you to work away from your computer, answer phone calls anywhere and list on more than one rental site.

Create an inventory checklist

Making a simple inventory checklist for yourself is a commonly overlooked task. This list will prevent you from accidently forgetting to stock, replace or provide necessities. You do not want to forget items like spoons, dish soap, toilet paper, remote batteries and so on. The list can also remind you to water plants, reset the temperature, and check easily to forget details.

Five Star Reviews

Another critical factor potential guests will consider when they are looking rent, is the rating that previous guests have left. In fact, this is one of the most essential features of the Airbnb community.

Having a high rating (four or five stars) will inspire confidence in future guests. This is what they rely on to make the best decision possible. No one wants to rent a place where the last three people declared their disgust with the services or amenities.

Get A Good Rating

Getting an excellent rating does not have to be complicated. Offer the kind of hospitality you would like to receive if you were traveling to a new town or city. Be helpful and welcoming to your guests. If possible, personally greet them when they first arrive. Therefore, even if you don't see them for the rest of their stay, you will have given them a good first impression.

As their stay progresses, check in with your guests to make sure they are comfortable and have everything they need. Also, try to collect the keys when they leave personally. This can be another incredible opportunity to make a connection with guests and remind them that you appreciate five-star reviews on Airbnb.

Go the Extra Mile

It's important to understand that your level of interaction will influence the number of tourists who will rent your property. If you want to create an Airbnb business that will earn you substantial profits, you have to offer extra services.

Short Cuts

Start by thoroughly reading the reviews left for the most popular listings, and learn from the feedback guest are giving. You should find at least a handful of tricks to make their stay extra amazing.

Don't stop there, also read all the bad reviews for issues that should be avoided. Once you have done your homework, use the information in the reviews to create a convincing listing. Mimic the positive reviews as close as possible to ensure a five-star experience.

Pick Them Up from the Airport

One of the best things you can do to make a first good impression is to pick up your guests at the airport. If you are not available or don't feel comfortable taking care of their commute, then provide information regarding transportation, taxi fees, bus and train connections.

Getting Around

Make a "welcome package" for your guests. Include a card with your contact details, a list of the best restaurant, museums, beaches, hiking, trails, grocery stores, and other exciting activities.

Personal Touches

Include personal touches in each room. Remember that guests are choosing Airbnb either for its affordability, amenities (like a kitchen), or its unique character. If you want to increase the asking price of your rental, do your best to capitalize on its unique characteristics.

Start by thinking of a signature special touch for the room or apartment. The room or home could be themed, modern, ecofriendly, or offer a beach feel.

A welcome package with information about your hometown is also a fantastic touch? A five start Airbnb experience often revolves around the unique details and personal touches.

Here is a list of items offered by top rated host.

- Bicycles
- Beach gear
- Golf carts
- Spa like experience
- Outdoor grilling
- Pick yourself gardens

- Organic linens
- Excellent mattress and pillows
- Spa-set
- Discounts to local attractions
- Hair dryer
- Soft robe
- Wind machine for better sleep
- Black out window coverings
- Movie channels
- Local coffee or tea and creamer, sugar
- Eco-friendly home
- Backyard campfire
- Tree house
- Garage parking
- Beautiful landscaping
- Air conditioning
- Cosy fireplace
- Ultra-comfy beds
- Themed rooms

- Rides to and from the airport

- Pet friendly

- Stocked refrigerator

- Children/infant supplies and bedding

- Pool or hot tub

- Close to tourist hot spots

- Properly heated and cooled

- Cooking oils

- Small cooler for use while they stay

Payment Guarantees

Is it possible for a guest to stay and not pay?

Fortunately, guests pay you through Airbnb. If there are no problems, Airbnb will release your payment within 24 hours of your guest's arrival. You should receive payment within a four-hours to a few days. However, those needing a check will have to wait up to 15 business days for a mailed check to be issued and arrive.

Guest Requesting Refund Rules

Guests must notify Airbnb within 24 hours of check-in if there's a problem that warrants a refund. If you don't respond to guests who try to contact you about an issue, they might be allowed to complete their reservation and receive a partial refund.

Airbnb could require you to refund a guest's payment if you cancel a reservation at the last minute, forget to leave the key, misrepresent your listing, don't clean your home or otherwise fail to meet Airbnb's hospitality standards.

Airbnb suggests making sure you're available within 24 hours of guests' scheduled check-in to address any concerns they might have since many problems are easily resolved. In your listing, make sure you describe your room type, number of bedrooms and bathrooms, and amenities accurately. If you choose to provide linens and towels, make sure they're clean. Also, notify guest if there will be any animals on the property.

Arranging Payment Outside of Airbnb

You could also get burned if you arrange payment with a guest outside of the Airbnb website. A guest might try to do this to avoid paying Airbnb's guest fee or might be planning to rip you off. As a host, you only stand to save 3% by not going through Airbnb's payment system, plus Airbnb could refuse to do further business with you if you get caught. So, don't try to circumvent the system, its simple not worth it.

Advertiser Disclosure

You'll want to clean and declutter your space before you photograph it to present it in the best possible light. In most cities, Airbnb will even send a professional photographer to capture your space for free if you're an active host.

When describing your place, think about what makes it unique, and try to consider it from an out-of-town visitor's point of view. Is your location within walking distance of public transit? Is it located near great restaurants, convention center, nightlife, beach, hiking, shopping, tourist sites, or cultural activities? What amenities can you offer: wireless Internet, a fully stocked kitchen, cable television, video games, hot tub, pool, fire pit, view, an outdoor patio?

Your listing will be displayed on Airbnb's website, and you can also cross-promote it through social media or your own website. If you are interested in making this your full-time business, building a great site will allow you to advertise and market independently. However, this is not required to make excellent money, stress free.

Pricing

Transparency

Now we're left with the emphasis on transparency and pricing. The heart of mastering these points is to keep it real. Don't claim to be something you're not, be honest and authentic. The last thing you need is a guest who felt lied to, and their horrible, painstakingly detailed review.

Your pricing strategy must reflect the reality, quality, and amenities of your property. You're not a hotel, and presenting yourself like one could be a huge turn off. Be practical about how you price your listing, while still staying aware of the competition. There are some strategic approaches to hitting the nail on the head with this one, as well as some internal Airbnb features that help lead you in the right direction. The most successful Airbnb host bare it all, while highlighting the properties unique characteristics.

Pricing Recommendation

Airbnb does recommend setting a price lower than your competitors until you have three positive reviews on your property.

Contact Me

A successful host always asks people to contact them. This is an excellent way for you to build a relationship with a potential guest and increase your likelihood of a booking.

In many cases, a single question is the only thing stopping a guest from saying yes. This may be due to an incomplete listing, strange wording, lack of details, or an individual request. In any case, increase your odds with a clearly worded "contact me."

Tracking Expenses

To be a successful host you will need to track all expenses and personal time put towards your individual properties or spaces. When you are offering something that is yielding a loss, the problem can be mitigated quickly. By adequately tracking your expenses, you will have the ability to reach higher profits.

Tracking your expenses will include all time and money spent on the property. If you are only renting out a room, then track the bills by square feet.

For example, the room is 300 square feet, and the entire home is 2000 square feet. Take 300 divided by 2000 to get 15%. This means that 15% of all your housing bills will need to be tracked as a part of your hosting expenses.

The actual expenses will be taken at face value. This could be toiletries, linens, beverages, replacement cost, cleaning services, etc.

Be Time Committed

If you are serious about making a profit through Airbnb, then you'll need to invest a few hours or more every week. You need to be constantly online and available to interact with your potential guests in real time.

Many times, you will have to communicate and answer questions regarding the accommodation you can provide, before a person is convinced to rent your space. You'll have to come up with a system to check guests in and out. Not to mention, you'll also have to manage cleaning, whether you choose to do it yourself or hire a specialized service.

Preparation Guidelines

Airbnb also provides guidelines for hosts to make their homes safer. If basic human decency doesn't give you enough incentive to make your place safe for guests, minimizing safety risks to guests reduces your risk of being sued by a guest who becomes injured on your property.

Guests will likely give you lower ratings if you haven't taken necessary precautions to protect them. This may result in things such as installing smoke and carbon monoxide detectors and eliminating any trip or fall hazards. If you're particularly negligent, Airbnb could refuse to let you continue to host.

Setting Up the House

One of the first things you need to do to impress your guests is to take their desires and expectations into consideration when setting up the space. Also, do not overlook the possibility of a guest getting injured.

Don't overcrowd the space, instead choose minimalistic decorations. Then you don't have to worry so much about items getting broken or affected by your visitors. Simple pieces of furniture will work just fine. Keep the furniture size in line with the size of the home. Larger furniture will make the space feel much smaller and less desirable.

I have compiled a list of does and don'ts that successful hosts strictly follow.

Do These Things

- Keep well stocked with toiletries
- Thoroughly clean after each guest
- Offer spaces free of clutter and oversized furniture

- Have enough table settings for at least the number of guest the property sleeps

- Clean windows of all prints and smudges

- Keep a well-groomed lawn

- Offer a complete welcome package

- Add fresh flowers to the table

- Have non-toxic indoor plants

- Post emergency numbers in plain sight

- Provide a map of the town or tourist hot spots

- Remove stains from furniture, carpets, doors, windows, and walls

- Provide salt and pepper, coffee, tea, creamer sugar, and cooking oil

- provide a few allergen free snacks for your new guest in addition to normal ones

- Have a few bottles of cold water in the refrigerator

- Child safe all outlets

- Repair potentially dangerous areas of the property

- Offer two sets of keys and keep a spare hidden or easily accessible
- Provide good quality linens, towels, blankets and pillows
- Launder linens with allergen sensitive detergents and fabric softeners
- Use mattress protectors
- Have a well-stocked kitchen
- Television, movies, games, and internet
- Good quality card and board games
- Offer an outdoor grill with supplies if possible

Don't Do These Things

- Leave kitchen appliances dirty
- Not professionally cleaned
- Leave exposed wire
- Only one key
- Leave torn or worn linens, mattresses and pillows
- Handprints and smudges

- Tile with poor grout, mildew or mold

- Cracked or dirty dishes in cupboards

- Home not properly stocked

- Low toilet paper supplies

- Cluttered spaces

- No toilet plunger

- No entertainment, tv or internet

- Strong deodorizing smells in: perfume, detergents, soaps, plug-ins or candles

- poor heating and cooling options

- inadequate water heating unit

- No cold water in refrigerator

- Unrepaired items

- Old television set

- Lack of operating instructions to appliances, heating and cooling, television, internet and more

- No welcome package

Super Charge Your Cleaning

Take the time to scrub the entire house before your guests arrive. Clean the kitchen, the hallways, the bathroom, and every space where your guests will have access. An unclean environment is what kills many Airbnb hosting careers.

If a few months have passed since your last booking, refresh your home, even if you've already cleaned the location after your previous guests.

Most Common Guest Complaints

Don't miss these items:

- Vacuum the carpets and mop your floors

- Cobwebs

- Not enough lighting, burnt out lightbulbs

- Wipe the countertops and remove furniture stains

- Thoroughly clean windows, sliding glass doors and walls

- Make your bathroom squeaky clean. Clean the sink, the bathtub, and the toilet, plunger, toilet bowel scrubber, shower curtain, and trash can

- Look for spider webs

- Fix hazards

- Leave no wire exposed, no step loose and no furniture broken. Fix anything that might injure a person

- Clean out the refrigerator. Make sure there's fresh water in the fridge for when they first arrive

Toiletries Make a Difference

It's a great idea to provide toiletry such as two bath towels per guest, lots of toilet paper, hand soap, shampoo, conditioner, body wash, toothpaste. Be sure to purchase items that are hypoallergenic and great for sensitive skin.

The last thing you want is a guest rushed to the hospital because of your bathroom soaps.

Replace Old Sheets with Fresh Ones

This advice might seem redundant for some people. However, you'll be shocked at how many hosts fail to follow this basic rule.

You must change and clean bed sheets after each guest. Buy some extra sets if you don't want to bother with cleaning bed sheets every week. It's a simple investment that will help you avoid bad reviews.

Also, do not reuse worn out bedsheets. This will disgust a guest and ensure a lousy review. Since bedsheets are a hot topic for a host, purchase sheets that are ultra-soft and easy to wash to minimize guest dissatisfaction.

Excellent bedding, and a good night's sleep is essential to a five-star review.

Key Exchange

Never provide a visitor with your only key. The key exchange is the first guest-host contact, so try making it as comfortable and pleasant as possible. Remember that your goal is always to get a positive review, so you need to create a smooth experience for your guests.

Live in a Big City?

If you are providing accommodation in a major city, the chances are that your guests will arrive at different times. The important thing is that someone should greet your guests, or the key must be available, no matter their arrival time. You wouldn't get positive feedback if your guests had to sit around and wait for you.

Meet and Greet Issues?

What if I am unable to meet the guest and deliver the key? A common key exchange solution is leaving your key with someone who stays nearby. This could be a friend, a relative or a neighbour.

Give your guests the number of the person responsible for the key and make sure that your friends are available to meet and greet the guests.

This method works best if you compensate your key-deliverer for their trouble.

Use a Key Box

A straightforward and efficient option is installing a lockbox with a simple code that you can share with your guests. That way, they can always have access to the key, no matter the hour of their check-in. You can either put it directly on the front door or hide it around the exterior of the house to keep it private from neighbours.

A smart lock is the most convenient method for both the host and the guest. You can also install a digital lock that you can control remotely via your mobile device. Or you can pass the code to your guests and change it every time they check out.

Drop the Key to a Nearby Shop

Another method is to drop the key to a nearby shop or cafe from where guests can quickly pick it up. This process requires having total confidence in the staff of the store to be responsible and attentive. However, make sure that your guests arrive during business hours.

The Importance of Privacy

Getting on Airbnb as a host means entering a community where each member's privacy must be respected. If you have surveillance devices placed in your home for security reasons, make sure your guests are aware by making it very clear in your housing description. Otherwise, the guest will have the right to cancel the reservation and ask for the refund while you, might have to deal with penalties.

With the advent of small spying devices, guests are getting worried that they may fall victim. It is essential to remove any devices from bedrooms or bathrooms that resemble spying or listening technology. This does not include the television.

Authenticity

The details about your house should be accurate and correct. If not, your low ratings will alert both future guests and Airbnb that you are not suitable to continue as a host.

Your responsibility is to provide an accurate description of the house, real images, and ensure that all standards have been met. Meaning correctly working electricity, heat, running water and cleanliness.

Get Positive Reviews

To get positive reviews, you need to follow these rules of success.

Always Update Your Availability

keep a very organized calendar, so that the platform knows when your space is unavailable.

Communicate promptly

make yourself available for your guests and be ready to share information about the housing, the check-in/check-out hours, and other issues, so that everyone's experience is five stars.

Be committed to reservations

Always get the accommodation ready before your guests arrive. If, for some reasons, you need to cancel the reservation, make sure your guests have enough time to find another place to rent.

Be accurate

Share only real information and set clear expectations regarding the services you are offering, and price your home Otherwise, your account can get suspended.

Creating A Perfect Listing

Listing a property on Airbnb is easy. The platform is user-friendly and straightforward, allowing you to upload your listing in no time. But if you want to stand out in the crowd, there are a few tips to follow.

Your Profile

Your profile represents one of the most critical elements of your Airbnb account. It has the power to convince a traveller that you are worthy of their trust and money. Complete your profile details as thoroughly and transparently as possible. Let visitors know what to expect from you as their host.

Your Title

Many people underestimate the importance of a catchy title.

Example:

1. "Swimmers paradise two-room apartment close to the beach."

2. "Cottage dream with pick-your-own garden."

3. "Modern studio apartment in the heart of town."

4. "Sleep under the stars in a custom tree-house."

Whatever you choose, make sure it is easy to remember. You don't need to specify the name of the city in your title, as tourists get to your listing after preselecting the location. However, if your house is located in the suburbs, downtown, or by something special you should mention that in the title.

Your Description
Here are the rules of an excellent description.

1. make it clear,

2. compelling,

3. and above all, make it honest.

Give as many details as you can to help potential guests get an accurate idea of what you are offering.

Whatever you do, don't make false or exaggerated claims!

Your House Rules

Airbnb allows all hosts to set their own housing rules, so take the time to analyse whatever limits you want to impose on your guests. Take into account your needs, the tourists' expectations, as well as the general rules of your neighbourhood or HOA (home owners association).

For example, if you live in a quiet building with private entrance, specify the quite hours. Make it clear in your rules if smoking is allowed in or outside the premises. Also, state the maximum number of people that can stay in your place, and if you allow visitors. In addition, let the guest know if they must perform specific house duties, such as taking out the garbage.

Your Images

The best Airbnb listings are the ones that have amazing photographs of the property. The logic is simple: the better the quality of the pictures, the higher the number of reservations requests. Guest will always select the home they feel is less risky.

Proper Lighting

Try to take well-lit pictures during the day, when you can emphasize the natural lighting. Choose the images that can give guests a better understanding of how the apartment looks, and how large it is, and the great experiences they can have in it. You should review the images of your more expensive competitors to see which angles they use to highlight the beauty of their property.

Airbnb Photography Services

The founders saw the dramatic change in the success that high-quality pictures brought to Airbnb hosts, which is why Airbnb offers free professional photography in a variety of cities to a variety of types of listings. Check and see if the services are available in your region.

High quality photos are the number one item which can consistently rent a property. It's all in the presentation. Your approach to your listing photography is indeed the bread and butter of a successful Airbnb business. And the company understands that.

Tricks High Earners Use

There is always something more that you could do to improve the overall experience for your guests. If your primary purpose is to obtain excellent reviews on the platform, then you should do everything you can to make your guests feel pampered.

Differentiate Yourself

Try to offer something unique to differentiate yourself from the competition: a meal to a restaurant, a free ride to a touristic sight, a jar of home-made cookies, locally grown coffee, towels folded like animals, etc. We guarantee that your guests will appreciate your effort and honour you with a five-star rating.

Ask for References

Beginnings are rough. The same stays true for your Airbnb career. If you are new to the platform, you may find it difficult to secure your first guest. People are usually looking for established places that have already been tried by travellers. They want to know what to expect and reduce the risk of a bad experience.

Get Friends to Write Reviews

Even if you are new to the platform, you can ask your friends and family to write five-star reviews. Have them "rent" at your place and leave you a review. You can offer them exclusive discounts or the lowest possible rate to persuade them to write great reviews about your accommodation and your skills as a host.

Handling a Bad Review

Sometimes, things can go wrong, even if you thought of everything. At the end of the day, nobody can please everybody 100% of the time.

No matter the circumstances of your new low rating, you must stay calm and handle the situation quickly and tactfully.

Responding

First, apologize to the guests for anything that was not up to satisfaction. Even if you don't agree with the feedback, hosting is a business and "the customer is always right." Let people know that you are genuinely feeling sorry for the bad experience, and you are doing everything in your power to fix the issues. This will help regain trust in your potential guest.

Guest Review

If you believe it was the customer's fault for the bad experience, remember that you have 14 days after the checkout to review the guest.

Public Response

If the feedback is devistating, write a public response to the review and explain what went wrong and how you are fixing it so that future guests don't experience the same problem.

Your reviews are permanent, so be professional in every aspect, from the way you treat your guests to the way you handle an online disagreement. Always acknowledge your fault and take your reviews as an opportunity to improve your property and the comfort of your future guests.

Communication

Don't forget that the best prevention of a bad review is excellent communication. By always staying in touch with your guests and assuring that they have everything they need, you can avoid low reviews. Many times, a bad review can come because of a misunderstanding. Therefore, keep in contact with your guests and solve their issues in real time.

List Property on Other Sites

Placing your property on other house-sharing increases your chances of having it booked on a regular basis. Airbnb is the largest and most popular platform in the world, but it's not the only one. Consider listing on HomeAway, VRBO, CHBO, and FlipKey to name a few.

Keep a very regimented schedule, so that you don't get yourself in the situation of having two reservations booked for the same period on two different platforms. Airbnb can import booking calendars from some other rental sites, so be sure to use this feature when possible.

Becoming an Airbnb Super Host

If you manage to grow your Airbnb business enough that you secure at least ten reservations in a year, you get a chance of becoming a Super Host. If hosts meet several benchmarks, they get the Super Host badge on their profile that ensures more visibility.

Super Host Requirements

1. You need to keep a high response rate of at least 90%

2. and have over 80% of your reviews be 5 stars.

Becoming a Super Host is not difficult, but you must impress guests with your hospitality skills. This requires time and dedication at the very least.

Everything must be in perfect order, starting with your presentation and finishing with the overall experience. As a super host that maintain this status for more than a year, you will receive travel coupons and are given priority support when calling Airbnb. Also, super hosts recieve invites to exclusive events.

Get Started Today

If you have a flair for hospitality and you are open to receiving strangers in your home, Airbnb can help you make extra money.

In the end, keep in mind that you must ensure that your guest's experience is enjoyable. It is also your responsibility to get into compliance with your local laws and regulations and make sure that your Airbnb activity is safe and legal for you.

Full Control

The great part about Airbnb is that you have complete control over the people you allow to rent your property. The platform allows you to refuse reservations and gives refunds if you feel that your guests are not respecting your desires.

Becoming a host on Airbnb is a real journey that can fulfil your life with incredible experiences, cultural exchange, and new worldwide connections.

www.ingramcontent.com/pod-product-compliance
Lightning Source LLC
Chambersburg PA
CBHW060137050426
42448CB00010B/2179